Theoretical Art
Movements

Theoretical Art Movements

Matthew Manus

iUniverse, Inc.
New York Lincoln Shanghai

Theoretical Art Movements

iUniverse, Inc.

For information address:
iUniverse, Inc.
2021 Pine Lake Road, Suite 100
Lincoln, NE 68512
www.iuniverse.com

ISBN: 0-595-32542-4

Printed in the United States of America

Contents

Introduction

This text is comprised of theoretical art movements that I conceived of while in isolation from other artists and art theorists.

Matthew Manus
Saint Louis, USA
July, 2004

Art-Abstinere

Art-Abstinere is a theoretical art movement where the artist intentionally refrains from creating the artwork.

Art-Accretion

Art-Accretion is a theoretical art movement where the artwork is continuously added to over time. For example, a painter might continuously return to a museum to add to a painting. This process would be seen as the artwork.

Ante-Art

Ante-Art is a theoretical art movement where the activities effectuated before the execution of the artwork are considered the artwork. For example, the preparations undertaken before sculpting would be seen as the artwork (as opposed to the sculpture itself).

Art-Aprés

Art-Aprés is a theoretical art movement where the activities conducted after the completion of the artwork are considered to be the artwork.

Artarchy

Artarchy is a theoretical art movement where a government is formed by practicing artists. The laws of Artarchy are aesthetic.

Artathonics

Artathonics is a theoretical art movement where the length of time put into the execution of the artwork is regarded as the artwork.

Art-Attrition

Art-Attrition is a theoretical art movement where the attrition of the artwork due to the natural elements is considered the work of art. For example, a painting in a museum might fade due to light and temperature. The fading of the painting would be considered the artwork.

Art-Brev

Art-Brev is a theoretical art movement where the work of art is left intentionally uncompleted.

Art-Cade

Art-Cade is a theoretical art movement where the display of the artworks is regarded as the artwork.

Art-Cel

Art-Cel is a theoretical art movement where the aesthetic aspects of the artwork are hidden or encrypted in non-aesthetic material.

Art-Class

Art-Class is a theoretical art movement where the arrangement of the materials is constantly recombined in new orders. This process of rearrangement is the artwork.

Art-Delecta

Art-Delecta is a theoretical art movement where the choices the artist makes in regards to the composition and form of the artwork are regarded as the artwork.

Art-Diction

Art-Diction is a theoretical art movement where what is said about the artwork is regarded as the artwork.

Art-Grade

Art-Grade is a theoretical art movement where the steps taken in the creation of the artwork are regarded as the artwork.

Art-Junct

Art-Junct is a theoretical art movement where the joining together of the elements of the artwork is what is regarded as the artwork. For example, the use of perspective and foreshadowing in a painting might be regarded as the artwork, rather than the painting itself.

Art-Medi

Art-Medi is a theoretical art movement where the empty space between the art-work and the viewer is regarded as the artwork. For example, while standing before a sculpture, the space between the viewer and the sculpture would be regarded as the artwork.

Art-Memento

Art-Memento is a theoretical art movement where the memory or memories of the artwork is regarded as the artwork. For example, after an art show, the memories of the artwork retained by the viewer would be seen as the artwork.

Art-Merc

Art-Merc is a theoretical art movement where the price value of the artwork is regarded as the artwork. For example, a price tag of one thousand dollars for a painting would be seen as the artwork.

Art-Mir

Art-Mir is a theoretical art movement where the act of viewing the artwork is regarded as the artwork.

Art-Od

Art-Od is a theoretical art movement where the path that the artwork takes through space is seen as the artwork. For example, a sculpture might travel from New York to London. The trajectory of the artwork through space would be seen as the artwork.

Artorama

Artorama is a theoretical art movement where all that can be viewed through the viewer's eyes is considered the artwork. For example, while looking at a painting in a museum, the viewer often sees other paintings, a wall, lights and other people. The view in its entirety is the artwork.

Art-Pulse

Art-Pulse is a theoretical art movement where the inner vision of the artist in regards to the artwork is regarded as the artwork.

Art-Reg

Art-Reg is a theoretical art movement where the rules that are applied in the execution of the artwork are regarded as the artwork.

Art-Relational

Art-Relational is where the relationship between the artist and the artwork is regarded as the artwork.

Art-Sci

Art-Sci is a theoretical art movement where what is known about the artwork and the materials and the artistic process of the creator of the artwork are regarded as the artwork.

Aster-Art

Aster-Art is a theoretical art movement where the imitations of the artwork are regarded as the artwork (as opposed to the original).

Auxiliary Art

Auxiliary Art is a theoretical art movement where the tools that are utilized in the execution of the artwork are regarded as the artwork. For example, the paintbrush and the paint and the palate utilized for the creation of a painting would be regarded as the artwork (as opposed to the painting itself).

Chron-Art

Chron-Art is a theoretical art movement where the artwork changes over time. The process of the artwork changing over time is seen as the artwork.

Color

Color is a theoretical art movement where everything that exists is seen simply as being comprised of color. Matter itself is simply 'color'.

Corrigation Art

Corrigation Art is a theoretical art movement where the corrections applied to the artwork are regarded as the artwork itself.

Distancialism

Distancialism is a theoretical art movement where the distance between the viewer and the artwork is regarded as the artwork. For example, there might be a distance of three feet between the viewer and the artwork. The three feet would be regarded as the artwork.

-Gade

-Gade is a theoretical art movement where the forces of attraction and repulsion in relation to the artwork are considered to be the artwork. For example, a viewer might like a painting. This relationship between the viewer and the painting is considered the artwork.

Holo-Art

Holo-Art is a theoretical art movement where the artwork is comprised of the artwork itself, the environment the artwork is sustained in and the viewer's perceptions of the artwork and the environment.

Hyperconstruction

Hyperconstruction is a theoretical art movement where the artist creates only one artwork for the entirety of his/her life.

Imaginality

Imaginality is a theoretical art movement where the Universe is seen as a work of art.

Incept-Art

Incept-Art is art that is begun but is never finished. For example, a painter might paint the beginning of a painting but leave it unfinished. That is an example of Incept-Art.

Intermath

Intermath is the aesthetic exploration of the relationship between the qualitative and the quantitative. For example, it might be possible to calculate mathematically for an aesthetic experience. This is what Intermath explores.

-Izm

-Izm is a theoretical art movement where everything that exists is seen as an art-work. For example, the sky might be seen as art, as might equally a painting.

Metricism

Metricism is art that is comprised of mathematical symbols. For example, there might be sculptures of numerals with mathematical titles.

Negative Art

Negative Art is a theoretical art movement where the artwork is created with the intention of not being perceived as art.

Palin-Art

Palin-Art is a theoretical art movement where the artwork looks the same when viewed from any given position or perspective.

Physio-Art

Physio-Art is a theoretical art movement where the conceptualization of new laws of nature, whether true or not, is seen as the artwork. Physio-Art is the intertwining of art and science.

-Style

-Style is a theoretical art movement where everything is seen through the lens of fashion. For example, clouds would be seen as part of the sky's fashion, and color would be seen as part of a painting's fashion.

Super-Art

Super-Art is a theoretical art movement where those aesthetic qualities that are not present in the artwork are regarded as the artwork. For example, a painting might leave out the color green. The color green would then be regarded as part of the artwork.

Teleconstruction

Teleconstruction is a theoretical art movement where the viewer creates the artwork from the materials chosen by the artist.

Ultraconstruction

Ultraconstruction is a theoretical art movement where the artist creates artworks that are intentionally beyond the understanding of the viewer.

Unconstruction

Unconstruction is a theoretical art movement where the artwork is dismantled into its original components. This process is the artwork.

www.ingramcontent.com/pod-product-compliance
Lightning Source LLC
Chambersburg PA
CBHW021040180526
45163CB00005B/2213